youth ministry CLIPART

Written and Illustrated By
Dave Adamson and Steve Hunt
of
The Church Art Works™

Group Books

Loveland, Colorado

Thanks to our staff: Kristen, Kelley, Rick, John and Ken. Additional thanks to the hundreds of youth workers who've helped us with ideas and encouragement. Our special thanks to Kim Doud and Ralph Rowland, who have consistently directed others to our work. We're all better because of their sharing spirit.

Youth Ministry Clip Art

Credits
Edited by Lee Sparks
Cover design by Judy Atwood and Steve Hunt
ISBN 0931-529-26-3

17 16 15 14 13 12 11 10 9 8   03 02 01 00 99 98 97 96 95 94

Printed in the United States of America.

Contents

Introduction

"John" is a youth worker: busy, on-the-go and usually behind in his paper work. John typically leads youth meetings, Bible studies and volunteer training. He also plans programs, makes phone calls and spends time just listening to the kids in his youth group. He sends out letters and publicity fliers for the events he wants to advertise. He wants these handouts, newsletters, fliers and posters to look "with it," but he lacks both the time and skill necessary to design sharp-looking materials. Then someone suggests that he use clip art. John asks, "What's clip art?"

Clip art is artwork that's already prepared. It is better than stick figures, but not quite custom-made. All you have to do is plan your publication and decide what you want to say. Then choose the artwork that best illustrates your idea, clip it and attach it to your planning sheet to be duplicated.

Newspapers and advertisers have used clip art for years as a quick, economical way to add interest to communication pieces. Until recently, this method of illustration was not as widely used by churches because of the limited capabilities of mimeograph machines. With the advent of the photocopier, churches have improved their printing methods and discovered clip art as a great tool for enhancing their publications.

When we began The Church Art Works in 1984, our goal was to produce contemporary graphics that today's youth could relate to with real enthusiasm. The religious clip art produced in secular publications was generally stale and stereotyped. The peaceful shepherd and the angelic cherub lacked relevance to the changing scene of today's youth ministries. We've tried to bridge the gap by providing contemporary illustrations for both traditional and creative ministry themes. If our mail is any indication of success, we feel we are accomplishing our goal. Youth workers from nearly every state and several foreign countries have written to say, "Now my kids *read* their mail!"

Within this book we have tried to provide a variety of subjects for all aspects of your youth ministry. The first chapter focuses on holidays and special events, ranging from a New Year's lock-in to Christmas communion. It also supplements the typical school calendar by referring to spring break, graduation and summer vacation.

The second chapter offers illustrations that relate to almost any spiritual topic your group might want to explore. These topics include cults, peer pressure, self-esteem, temptation, prayer, God's will and several others.

The emphasis for the third chapter is recreation and includes planned activities such as bike hikes, ski trips, retreats and camps. The fourth

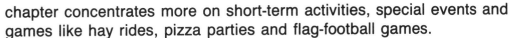

chapter concentrates more on short-term activities, special events and games like hay rides, pizza parties and flag-football games.

The chapter on zanies offers a myriad of illustrations like ears, hands and weird characters that could draw attention to all kinds of information within your publications. The fund-raiser chapter provides delightful ideas to promote your mission project, canned-food drive or car wash. And the last chapter provides numerous ready-made borders and forms to further enhance your publications.

We hope you'll find this resource book a helpful assistant to your youth work. It represents a collection of the best illustrations from our first two volumes of The Church Art Works™ clip art. By offering our clip art in book form, we have attempted to provide the same good product in a form conducive to heavy use.

As you thumb through these pages, you'll see that quality has also been our goal. We've spent a lot of warm summer nights at the office working and reworking ideas because we refused to be satisfied with anything less than our best. We hope you feel the same commitment to your work with teenagers. Young people are worth our investment.

Dave Adamson and Steve Hunt

Editor's Note:
For more information and brochures on other products and services by The Church Art Works™ including:
- Clip art,
- Custom art design services,
- One Way Out Shirts™ (Christian theme T-shirts),
- Custom T-shirt design and printing,

Contact: The Church Art Works™
875 High St. NE
Salem, OR 97301
(503) 370-9377

How to Use This Book

The clip art in this book will inject energy into and attract attention to your communication efforts such as newsletters, bulletins, fliers, posters, mailings, etc. Some of the illustrations are designed to advertise and emphasize specific activities. Therefore, some of the ideas in this book may stimulate an idea for your group as well as offer the art to promote it.

We realize that many of you will not always have the time or the energy to follow these directions carefully. There will be times when you merely "eyeball" your work in order to get it out on time. This section provides hints on how to produce a quality product, to go beyond the make-do type of communication piece. You can use the following steps to design any type of communication piece, but for our purposes we will use these steps to design a flier.

Let the space in Diagram 1 represent a sheet of blank 8½×11 paper that you will use to prepare a flier. You may choose to make your message as crowded or airy as you wish, depending on the amount of information you include. Remember, you're in control. Resist the temptation to jam the space with lots of items. Most is usually not best. Determine at the beginning just how much material will go into the available space.

1. *Plan carefully.* To avoid a haphazard project, ask yourself these questions as you plan: What's the *purpose* of this flier? What *type of audience* will read this material? What *information* needs to be presented?

2. *Write a rough draft of what you want to say on a piece of scrap paper.* Even though you think you will remember everything, write it down. This extra effort will help you

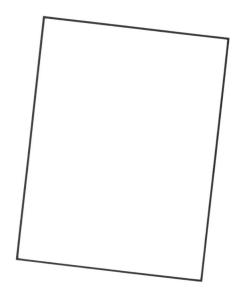

1. The blank page is the "space" you'll be working in. Remember not to crowd it

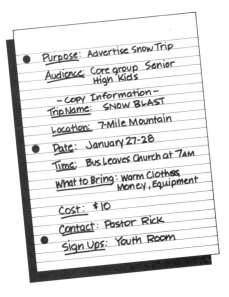

2. On a piece of scrap paper, list all the information your young people will need to know

visualize the content more clearly. Make sure your information answers the reader's questions: who, what, where, why, when and how. (See Diagram 2.)

3. *Rewrite your rough draft and edit your work.* Check to be sure you have included every detail your reader will need. Check for correct grammar, spelling and punctuation. Put your work aside and come back to it later. Then read it again. Is it clear and complete? Type your work and then proofread for errors.

4. *Picture the finished flier in your mind.* Will it appeal to the teenagers you are attempting to reach? Will its content encourage junior highers to give it a second glance? Will it stimulate the curiosity of your high school young people? Try to put yourself in your young people's place to see if this writing would appeal to you. If you need to change something, change it. As you work with your message and continue to edit it for your audience, you'll discover you've strengthened the thrust of your ideas.

5. *Think of a creative concept and design for your flier.* Decide if the flier will be traditional, humorous, formal, radical or thematic (like a jungle theme, snow theme, sports theme, etc.). The art should appeal to your young people. If the activity is a ski trip or tubing activity, make sure the border and illustrations suggest a winter atmosphere. Thumb through the clip art pages to find illustrations that fit the subject and character of your event. Notice the artwork is printed on only one side of the page. Use sharp scissors or an X-acto knife to clip the art

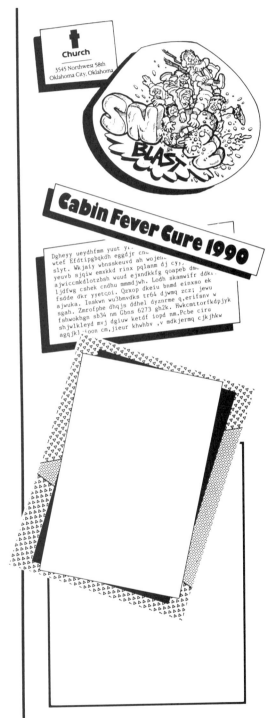

3. Gather all the elements you'll need for your flier. Make sure you have all the parts you need to tell the complete story.

you want to use. It's okay to leave some white space around the artwork.

Choose an appropriate and appealing headline. If your audience is primarily unchurched teenagers, make sure your headline avoids churchy language. A headline like "Follow the Leader" is much less threatening than "Lessons in Discipleship." If you need a headline that's not in this book, design your own. Have it typeset or use rub-on lettering available at most office supply stores. Use a T square and a triangle to make sure your copy is straight. If you have never worked with printed copy before, you may ask for basic lessons from some individual in your congregation who has experience with the graphic arts or drafting. (See Diagram 3.)

When designing your flier, try to assemble the following elements in this order: attention-getter, subtitle, block of copy and sign-off. The attention-getter can be an illustration and (or) the headline and is usually the largest item on the page. The subtitle adds additional, quick information and explains the attention-getter. The block of copy contains the detailed information you have carefully prepared, and the sign-off is usually the logo or name of the church with its address and phone number.

Remember, an attractive flier reflects a planned balance between these elements and the space around them. If your block of copy is too small, it will look lonely in a sea of white space. If the elements are too large, your flier will look crowded.

Lay out all the parts on top of a table and move them around like puzzle pieces to get your favorite layout. Rather than overlap edges of your paste-up pieces, trim them to fit. Overlapping tends to produce shadows that reduce the quality

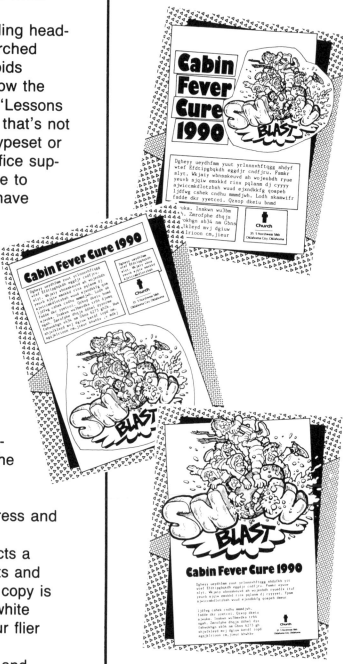

4. Move the elements around. Enlarge or reduce some of them to achieve a pleasing layout. If the block of copy needs to be redesigned to fit, retype that now.

of your work. (You might, however, overlap the art if it helps the design.) If adjustments need to be made in the copy to fit an irregular space, you can do this by editing copy or retyping it to fit the available space. You might also consider enlarging or reducing different elements to get the balance you want. (See Diagram 4.)

6. *Follow these steps to complete your flier:*

● Wash your hands carefully to remove all printer's ink or soil from your finger tips.

● Tape a blank piece of paper onto a clean table top or drawing board.

● Using rubber cement, paste your border first. This will allow you to "see" your outer boundaries and overlap your artwork, if necessary.

● Paste the headline and clip art to your paper. In the remaining space, paste your typed copy and logo items.

● Clean your completed work with correction fluid or an eraser. Be sure to remove all spots and fingerprints.

● Cover your work with another piece of paper to protect it from damage until it's printed or photocopied. (See Diagram 5.)

This extra effort may feel time-consuming and awkward at first. But after you have worked with the process a few times, you will realize anyone can do it. When you feel comfortable with most of these graphic-arts skills, ask your young people to help create communication pieces for their group's activities. Some kids in your church may have already learned basic paste-up skills by working on their school newspaper or the yearbook. Your decision to share this responsibility for quality communication with your young people will let them know you think they are "worth the investment" of your time and energy.

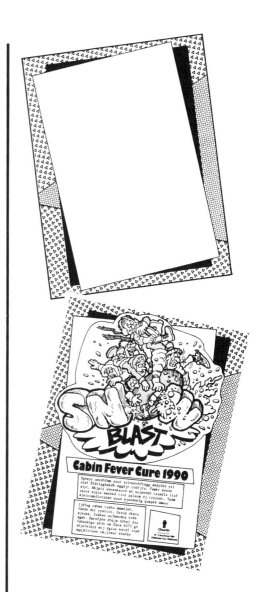

5. Paste up the border, attention-getter, subtitle, copy and logo in sequence. Then clean up the spots and fingerprints. Cover with another sheet of paper to protect your copy until you are ready to use it.

Holidays, Special Events

10

APRIL FOOLS

EASTER

He is Risen

GRADUATION

SCHOOL'S OUT!

GRADUATION

MOTHER'S DAY

FATHER'S DAY

SCHOOL'S OUT!

Summer
Celebration

Summer
Celebration

THE GREAT PUMPKIN CHASE

THE GREAT PUMPKIN CHASE

CHRISTMAS BANQUET

CHRISTMAS COMMUNION

CHRISTMAS PARTY

Shop'Till You Drop

Shop'Till You Drop

Spiritual Emphasis

22

PLAY IT BY THE BOOK

PLAY IT BY THE BOOK

YOU CAN BE A LIFE SAVER

Helping a Friend When His Life Goes Sour

CULTS
They Are Not What They Seem

CULTS
They Are Not What They Seem

CULTS
They Are Not What They Seem

PLAY IT BY THE BOOK

YOU CAN BE A LIFE SAVER
Helping a Friend When His Life Goes Sour

THANKS A LOT, GOD!

Learning to Like the Person in the Mirror

RATING YOUR DATING

God's Insights on Love, Sex, and Relationships

RATING YOUR DATING

God's Insights on Love, Sex, and Relationships

IS YOUR GOD TOO SMALL?

Expanding Your Concept of God

RATING YOUR DATING

God's Insights on Love, Sex, and Relationships

IS YOUR GOD TOO SMALL?

Expanding Your Concept of God

THANKS A LOT, GOD!

Learning to Like the Person in the Mirror

INNER BATTLES

HOW CAN YOU KNOW FOR SURE?

INNER BATTLES

WHAT HAPPENS WHEN I BLOW IT?

WHAT HAPPENS WHEN I BLOW IT?

HOW CAN YOU KNOW FOR SURE?

INNER BATTLES

WHAT HAPPENS WHEN I BLOW IT?

HOW CAN YOU KNOW FOR SURE?

THE VOICE OF THE CROWD

The Dilemma of Peer Pressure

TRUE BLUE

Insights on Making Strong, Lasting Friendships

YOU CAN MAKE A DIFFERENCE

YOU CAN MAKE A DIFFERENCE

WHAT HAPPENS AFTER DEATH?

FOLLOW THE LEADER

Lessons in Discipleship.

READY OR NOT, HERE I COME

Living in Anticipation of Christ's Return.

READY OR NOT, HERE I COME

Living in Anticipation of Christ's Return.

NEVER GONNA BE THE SAME

Your New Life in Christ.

MASTER CONTROL

Discovering God's Will for your Life.

MASTER CONTROL

Discovering God's Will for your Life.

NEVER GONNA BE THE SAME

Your New Life in Christ.

FOLLOW THE LEADER

Lessons in Discipleship.

Dealing With Temptation

l"EVER SAY DIE

Reinforcing my Commitment to God.

Possession Obsession

ABORTION?

MAKING
THE BEST DECISION

ABORTION?

MAKING
THE BEST DECISION

taming the tongue

taming the tongue

l... ...i...n O... ..i...

BUILDING SPIRITUAL STRENGTH

BUILDING SPIRITUAL STRENGTH

DIGGING DEEPER

DIGGIN' IN

RUN FOR THE PRIZE

RUN FOR THE PRIZE

DIGGING DEEPER

DIGGIN' IN

RUN FOR THE PRIZE

BIBLE STUDY

COUNT THE COST

COUNT THE COST

COUNT THE COST

World Christian Concern

the TIMOTHY Club

Programming Your Life

CAMPUS MINISTRY

CAMPUS MINISTRY

Programming Your Life

the TIMOTHY Club

the TIMOTHY Club

42

The Great Escape

The Great Escape

The Great Escape

BEACH TRIP

BackPack Attack

STAFF ATTACK

ADVANCE
(OPTIONS)
RETREAT

ADVANCE
(OPTIONS)
RETREAT

STAFF ATTACK

YOUTH ADVANCE

YOUTH ADVANCE

GRUB CAMP

GRUB CAMP

CAMP-OUT

Fellowship, Sports, Games

54

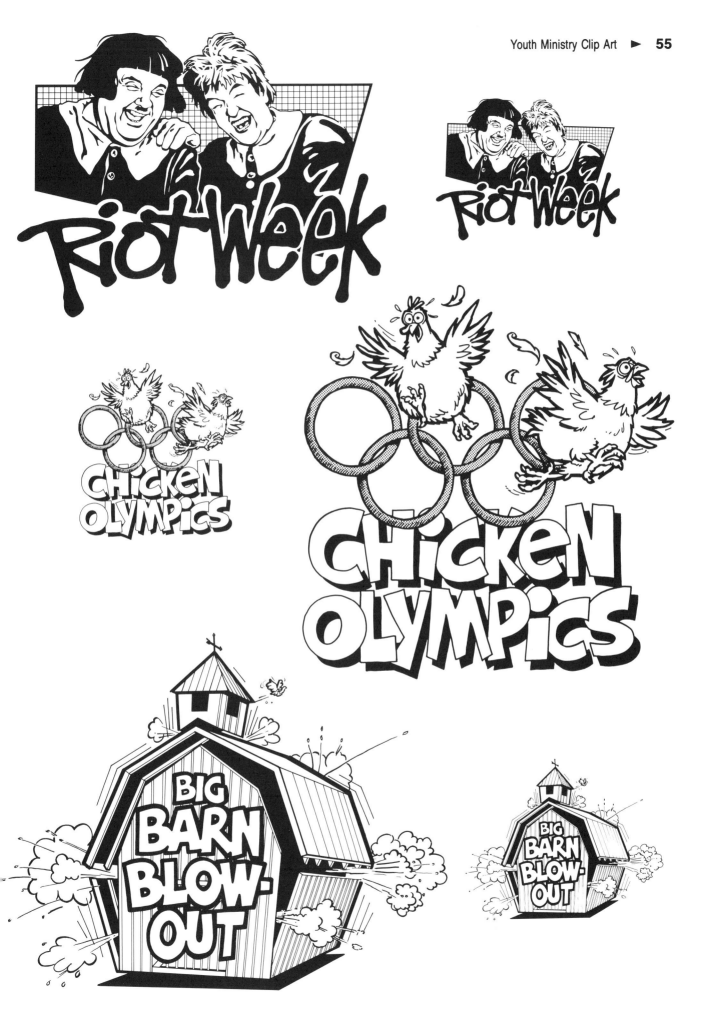

(Lungs Optional)

VIDEO NIGHT

NIGHT OF THE ASSASSIN

VIDEO NIGHT

NIGHT OF THE ASSASSIN

CLUE SEARCH

CLUE SEARCH

Miniature Golf

Miniature Golf

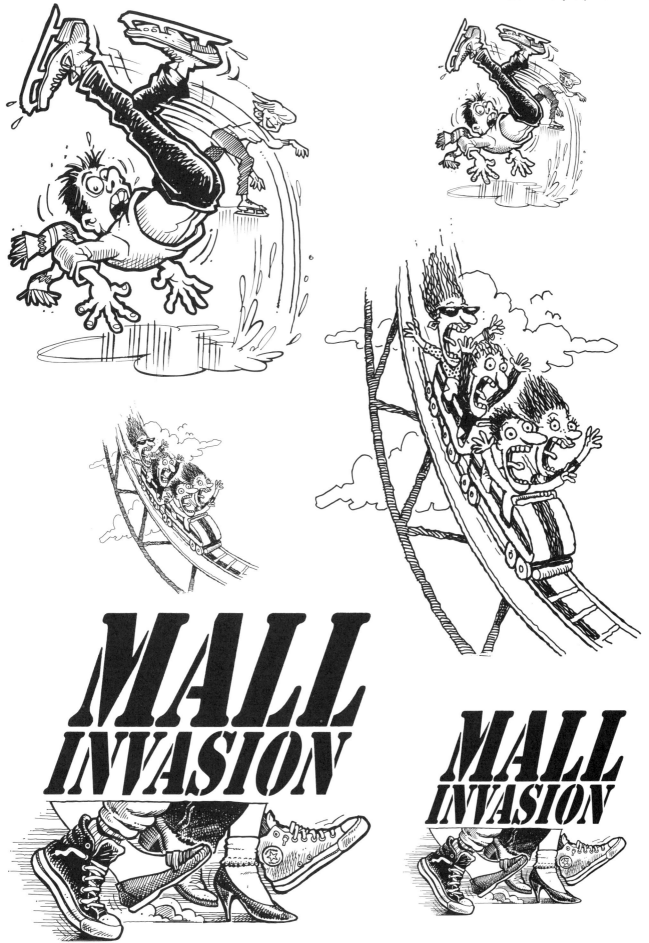

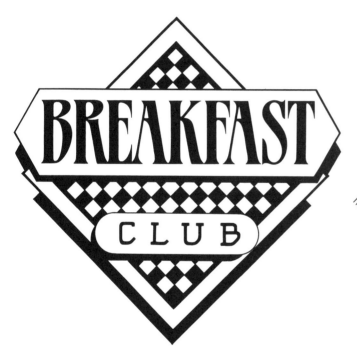

VIKING FEAST

VIKING FEAST

BURGER BASH

BURGER BASH

BROOM HOCKEY

BROOM HOCKEY

FRISBEE GOLF

FRISBEE GOLF

Ultimate Frisbee

Ultimate Frisbee

CRUISE'N BRUISE

Let the Good Times Roll

Let the Good Times Roll

Zany Characters and Situations

77

IN-TUNE

Bring A Friend!

Bring A Friend!

**Be There or
Be Square!**

**Be There or
Be Square!**

**Be There or
Be Square!**

Bring A Friend!

LOOKING AHEAD

LOOKING AHEAD

LOOKING AHEAD

Picture of Your Activity Here

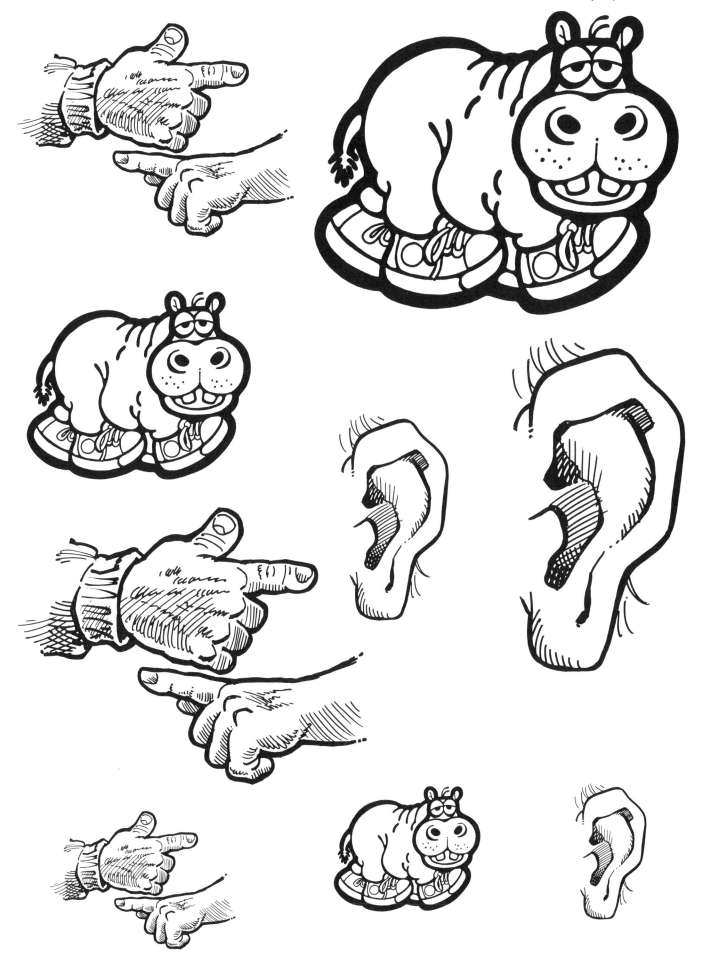

Fund Raisers

91

SPAGHETTI DINNER

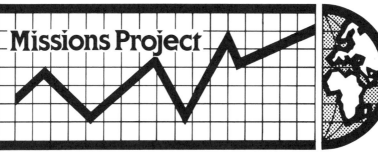

CANDY SALES

chili feed

CANDY SALES

chili feed

BOOK & GIFT SALE

BOOK & GIFT SALE

chili feed

PANCAKE FEED

CANNED FOOD DRIVE

CANNED FOOD DRIVE

PANCAKE FEED

Forms, Borders, Cards

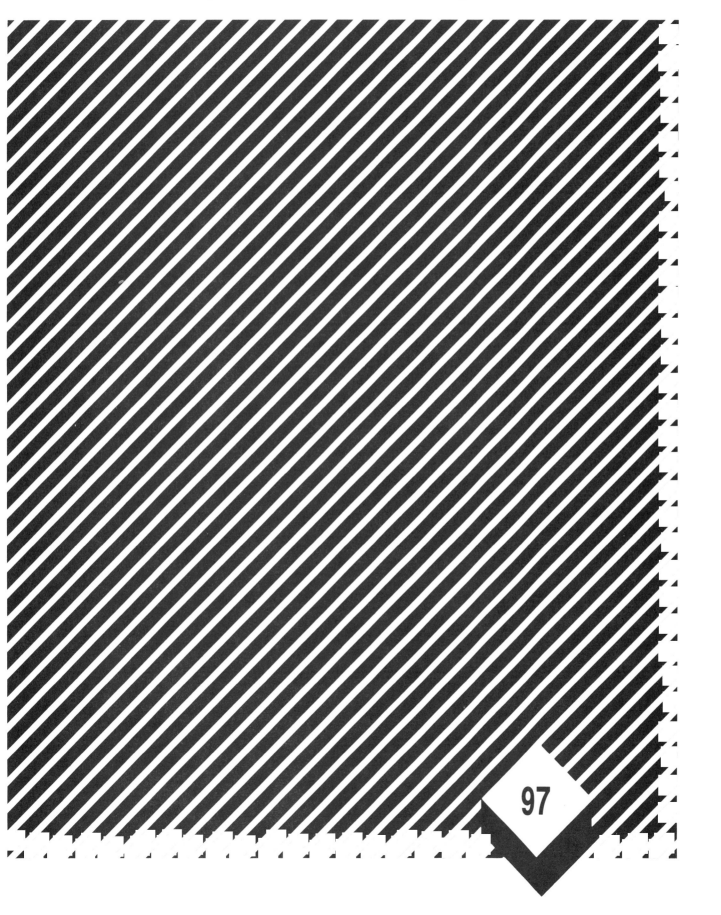

97

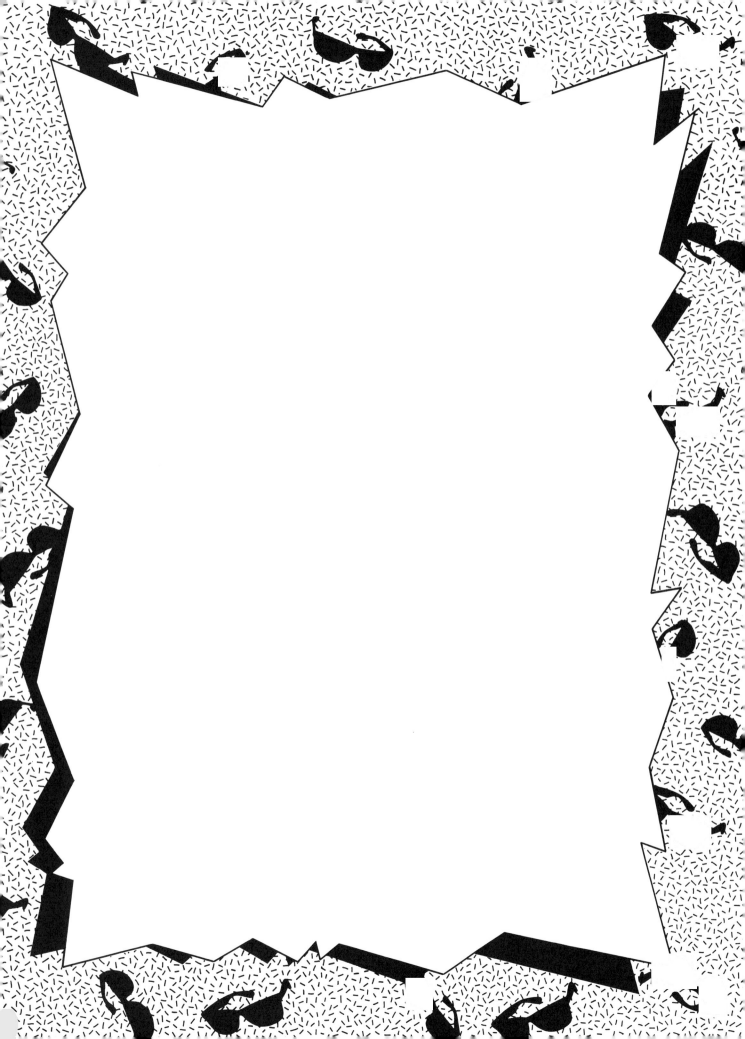

PLEASE NOTE:

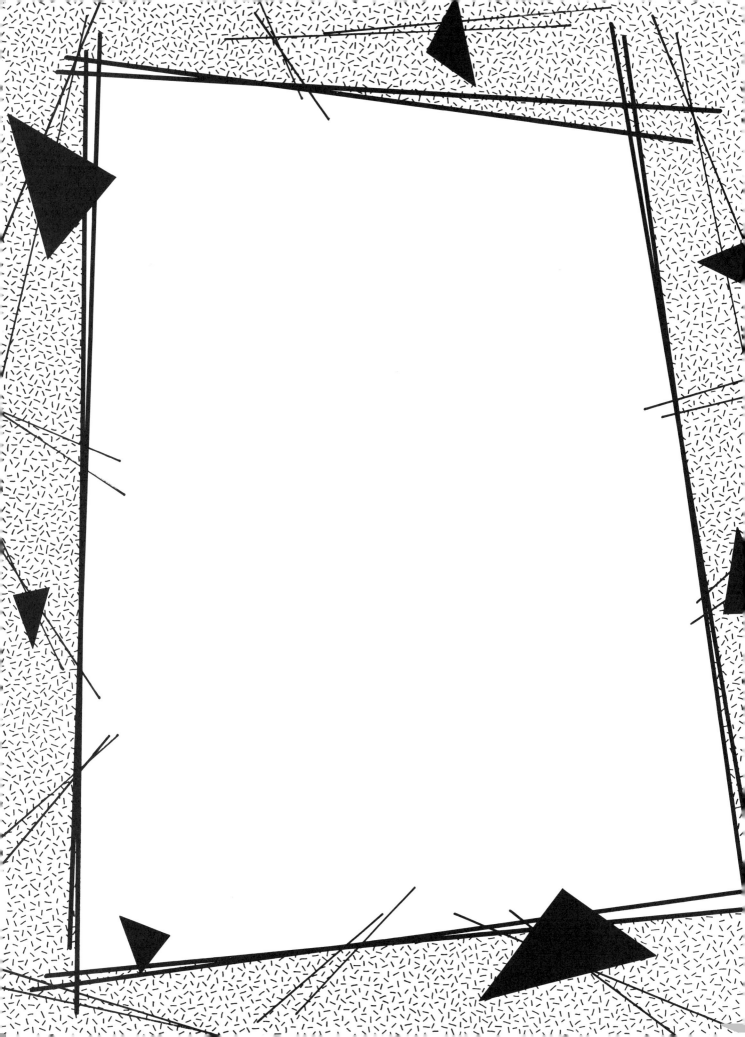

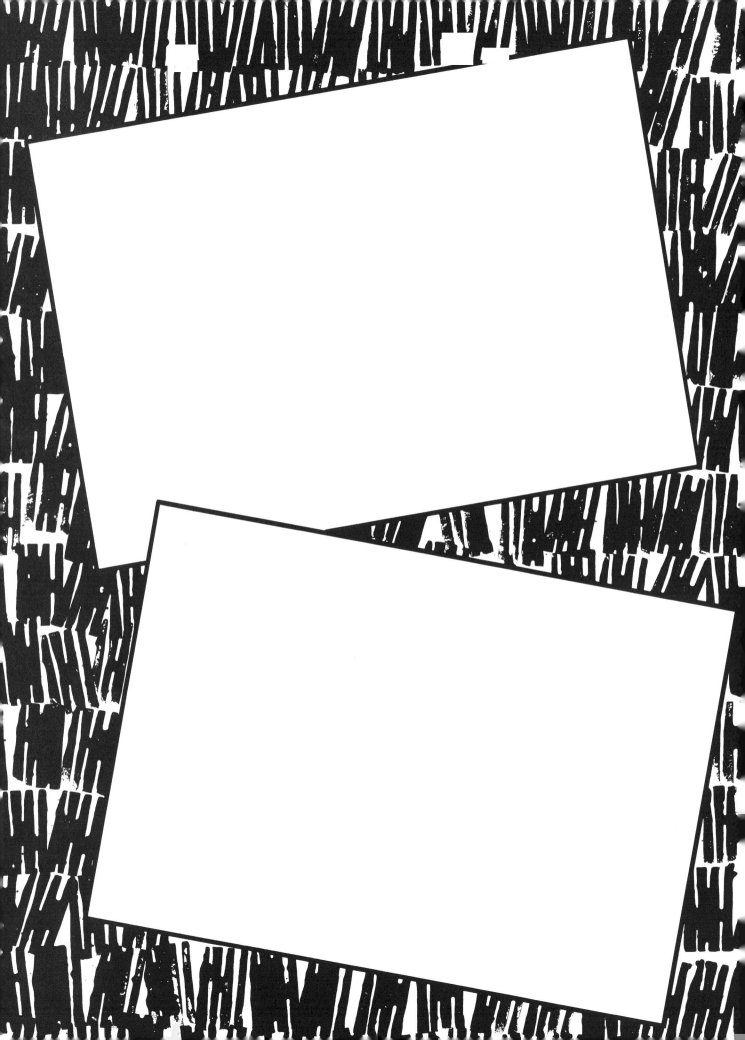

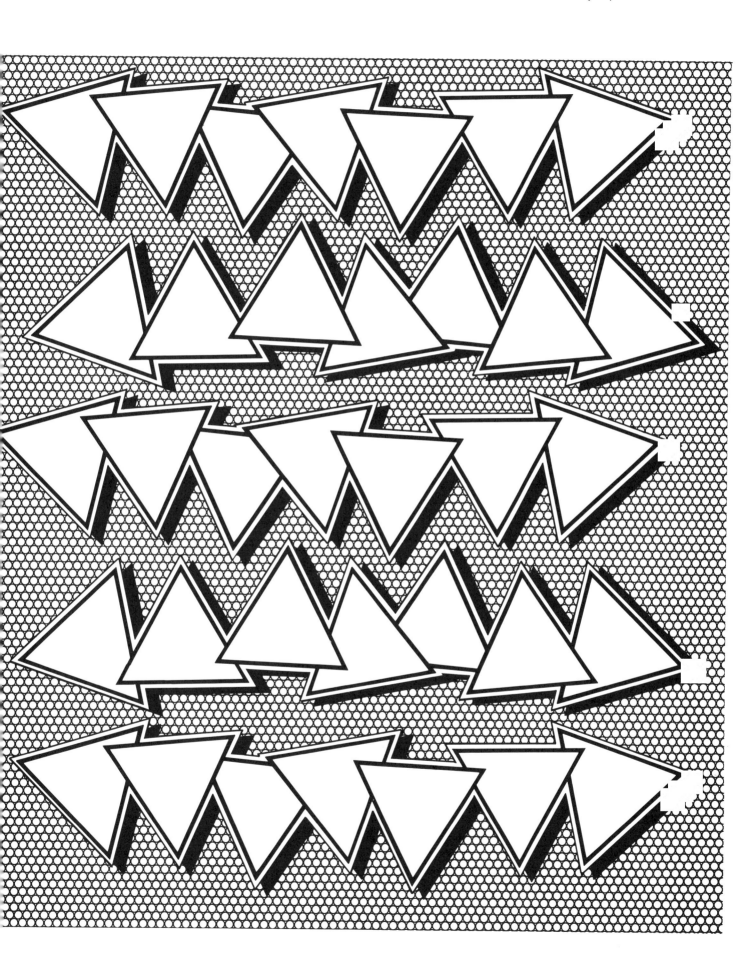

ActivityCalendar

SUNDAY	MON	TUES	WEDNESDAY	THURS	FRIDAY	SATURDAY

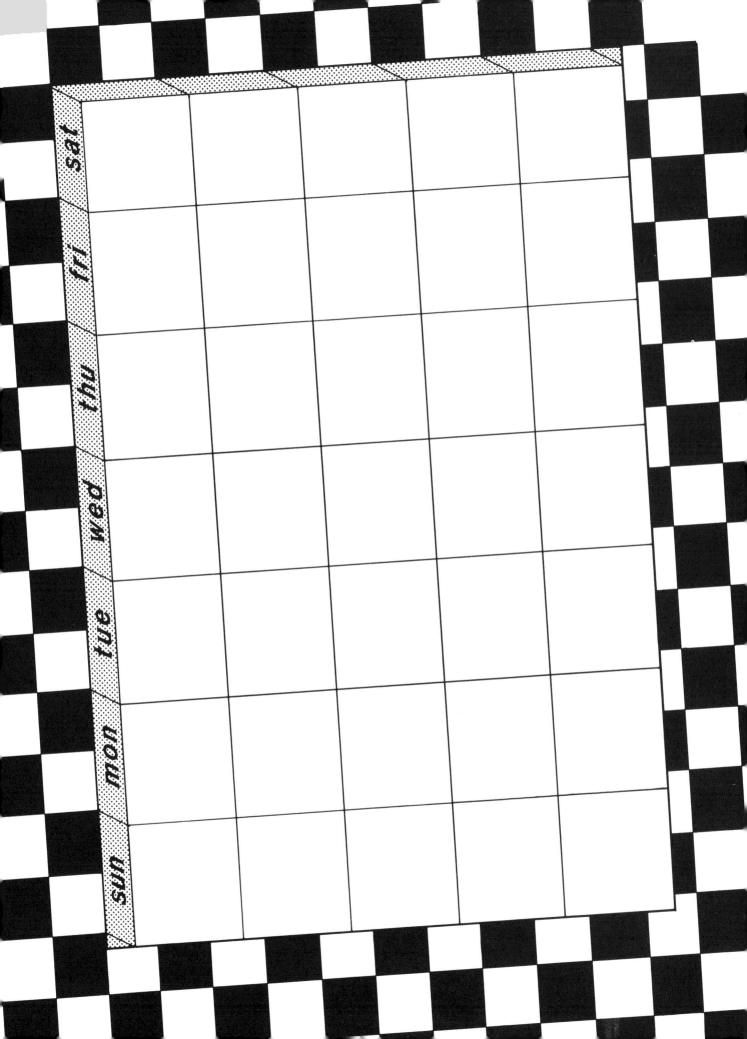

sat

fri

thu

wed

tue

mon

sun

JANUARY

FEBRUARY

MARCH

APRIL

MAY

JUNE

JULY

AUGUST

SEPTEMBER

OCTOBER

NOVEMBER

DECEMBER

January

February

March

April

May

June

July

August

September

October

November

December

or: _____ Date: _____ Time: _____

SIGN-UP SHEET

Name:

Name:

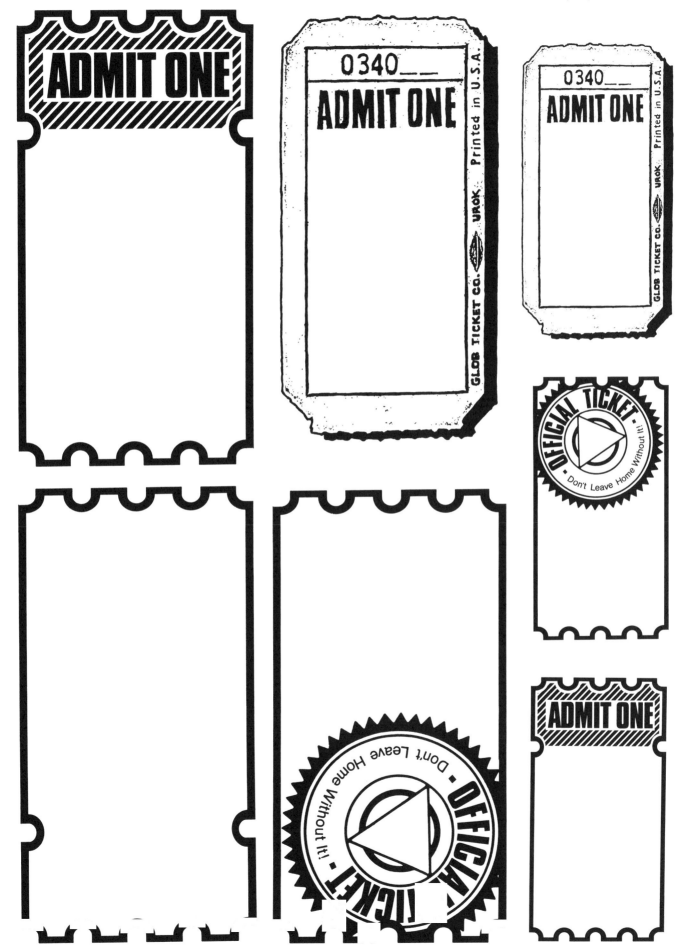

MEDICAL RELEASE

Name _____

Address _____

City _____ State ____ Zip _____

Phone _____

Person to Notify: _____

In the event of an emergency where medical treatment is required I give my permission to the church staff or sponsor to obtain the services of a licensed physician. Please attempt to notify me immediately concerning any such emergency.

Comments or medical info: _____

_____

Signed _____ Date _____
       (Parent or Guardian)

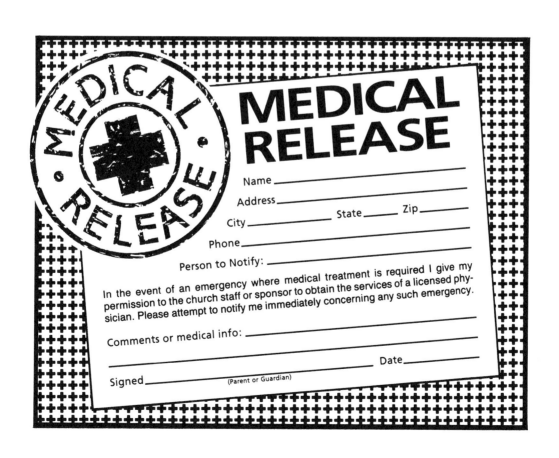

MEDICAL RELEASE

Name _____

Address _____

City _____ State ____ Zip _____

Phone _____

Person to Notify: _____

In the event of an emergency where medical treatment is required I give my permission to the church staff or sponsor to obtain the services of a licensed physician. Please attempt to notify me immediately concerning any such emergency.

Comments or medical info: _____

_____ Date _____

Signed _____
       (Parent or Guardian)

Fold 8½ x 11 into quarters.

Fold 8½ x 11 into quarters.

Fold 8½ x 11 into quarters.

SPECIAL SPEAKERS:
ARRIVING:
DEPARTURE:

WHAT TO BRING:

WHAT NOT TO BRING:

COST INCLUDES:

Jr. High   *Clubs*
Junior High
High School
College/Career
Middle School
Student Ministries

Jr. High   **Clubs**
Junior High
High School
College/Career
Middle School
Student Ministries

Jr. High   *Clubs*
Junior High
High School
College/Career
Middle School
Student Ministries

Jr. High
Junior High
High School **Clubs**
College/Career
Middle School
Student Ministries

notes&news

SPECIAL SPEAKER

notes&news

SPECIAL SPEAKER

You're Invited

Coming Events

Coming Attractions

This Week
Next Week
Sunday Nite

Believe It or Don't

Start Saving
Your Bucks Now!

Don't Be Late!

Don't Forget

Be There or Be Square!

You're Invited

Coming Events

Coming Attractions

This Week
Next Week
Sunday Nite

Believe It or Don't

*Start Saving
Your Bucks Now!*

KEEPING IN TOUCH WITH STUDENT MINISTRIES

KEEPING IN TOUCH WITH STUDENT MINISTRIES

Prepare Yourself...

Welcome

Get Psyched!

Outrageous!

RAD!

Sign Up

Welcome!

THANK YOU

Here's What's Happening...

Down the Road...

Sign Up Now!

Just A Note...

Coming Soon...

THANK YOU

THANK YOU

Sign Up

Register Now!

Prepare Yourself...
Welcome
Get Psyched!
Outrageous!
Here's What's Happening...
Bring A Friend!
Don't Be Late!
Don't Forget

Down the Road...
Sign Up Now!
Just A Note...
Coming Soon...

Register Now!

RAD!

ANNOUNCING

Welcome!

HELP WANTED

Sign Up

HELP WANTED

ANNOUNCING

Index